AF338133

SOUND AND LIGHT EXPERIMENTS FOR HANDS-ON LEARNING

SCIENCE 4TH GRADE

CHILDREN'S SCIENCE EDUCATION BOOKS

In this book, we're going to talk about some fun experiments you can do with sound and light. So, let's get right to it!

Hands-on experiments are interesting to do and a great way to learn about science. Make sure you have a science journal where you can record your findings. Also be sure there is an adult with you to supervise when you perform experiments either at home or at school. Safety first!

EXPERIMENT 1

SQUAWK LIKE A CHICKEN—A sound experiment

Things you'll need:

You'll need a drinking cup made of plastic. You'll also need a long piece of yarn. Cotton string can work too, but nylon won't work. You'll need a paper towel, a paper clip, a nail, some scissors, and water.

What to do:

Step 1: Use the scissors to cut a piece of yarn about 20 inches in length.

Step 2: Ask the adult who is helping to poke a hole in the bottom center of the cup using the pointy end of the nail.

Step 3: Take the paper clip and tie one end of the yarn to the middle of the clip.

Step 4: Take the other end of the piece of yarn and push it through the bottom of the cup. Pull it out the other side. If you've done it correctly the paper clip should be dangling near the bottom of the cup.

Step 5: Take a paper towel, about dollar-bill size, and get it slightly damp using some water.

Step 6: Now it's time to make your "chicken" squawk! Hold the cup with its bottom facing toward the ceiling and wrap your towel around the yarn close to the cup.

Step 7: Now, squeeze the string and pull it down in short, rhythmic jerks. The paper towel should slide down the yarn as you do your sequence of movements. If you do it right, you should hear your "chicken" squawking!

What this experiment shows:

Have you ever wondered how a piano or music box works? It works using the same principle as your plastic cup chicken. Without the cup, you wouldn't hear much noise if any when you move the paper towel on the yarn. However, the cup acts as an amplifier to "ramp up" the vibrations along the string.

EXPERIMENT 2

PLUCKING THE "STRINGS"—A sound experiment

You'll need a pencil box made of cardboard. You can set aside the lid. You'll need a bunch of rubber bands that have different thicknesses as well as different lengths. You'll need a ruler and some notebook paper.

Step 1: Organize your rubber bands from the thinnest to the thickest.

Step 2: Wrap each rubber band around the box on the long dimension, in order from the thinnest one to the thickest one. You're making what looks like the strings on a guitar.

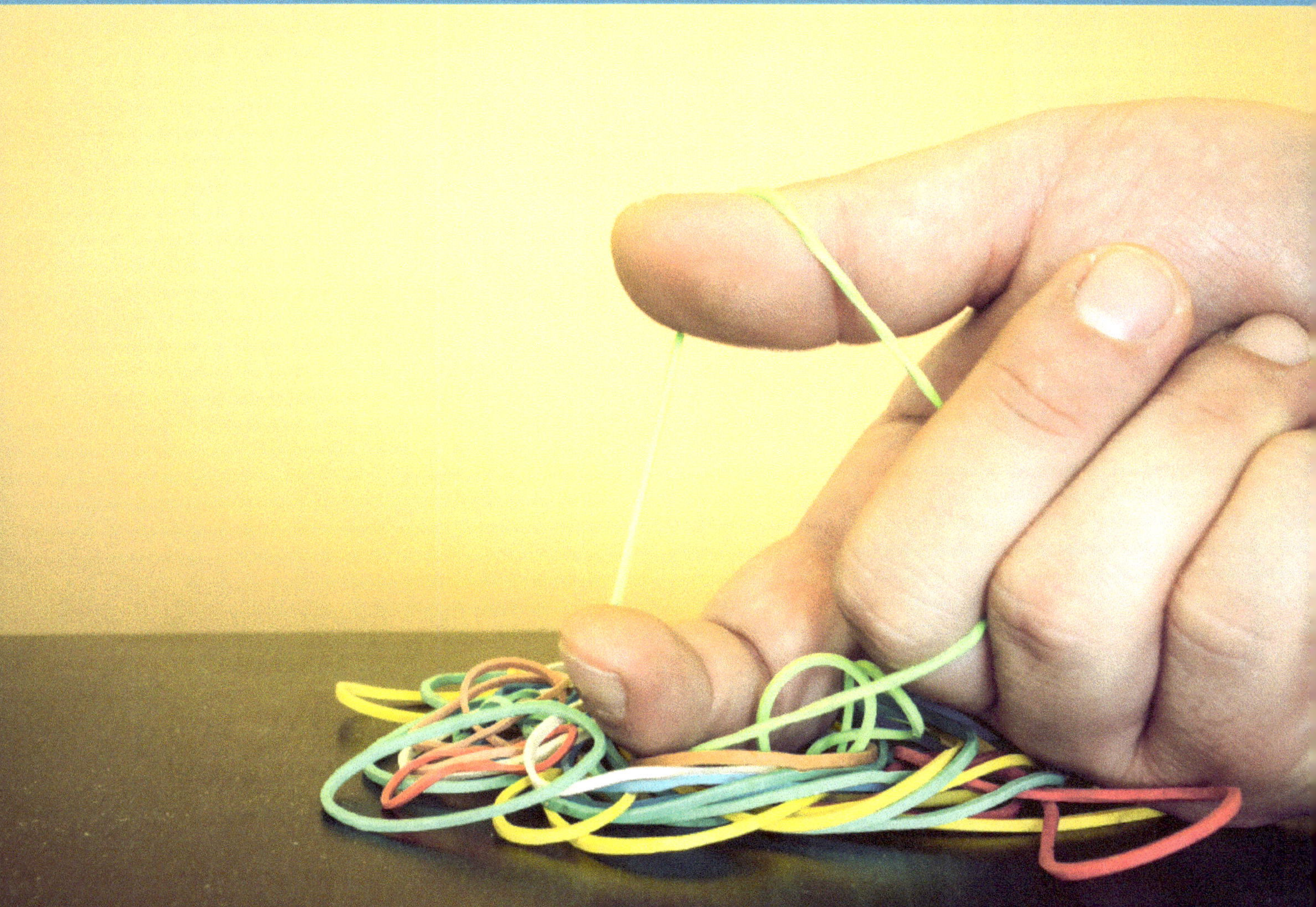

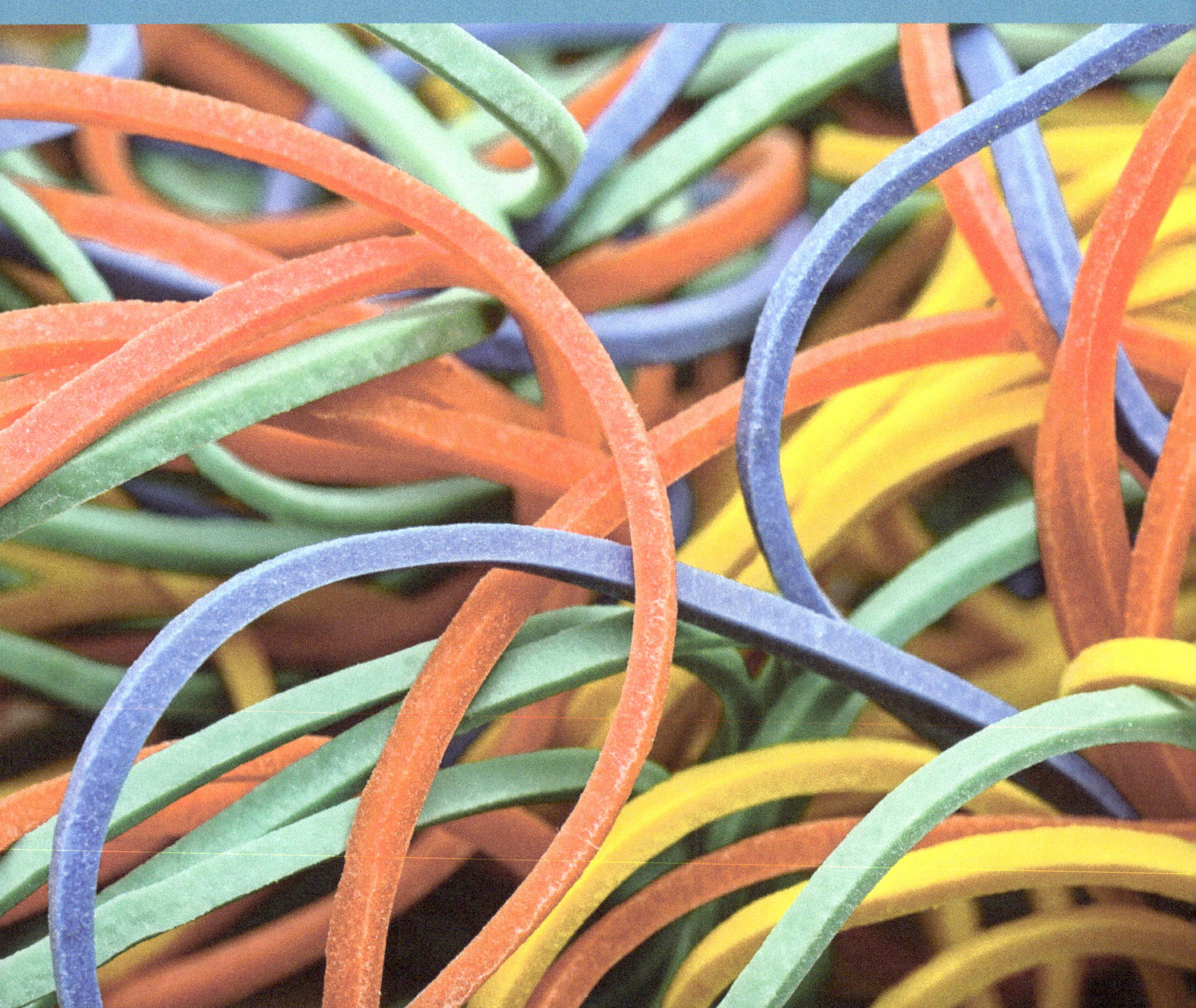

Step 3: Pluck the first band, then the second, and so on. Record your findings in your science journal.

Step 4: Now, place the ruler on its edge to form a bridge across the rubber bands in the center across the bands. The bands will become tighter as you press down.

Step 5: Repeat step 3 with the ruler in place and record your findings.

Step 6: Experiment with the ruler in different positions to the left or right to see how it impacts the sound when you pluck the different bands.

Step 7: Record your findings.

What this experiment shows:

If you've ever opened the top of a piano, you will have seen the strings inside. This experiment is based on the same principle. When you pluck the bands in Step 3 from the thinnest one to the thickest one, the sound vibrates differently depending on the thickness. It changes from a higher pitch to a lower pitch. When you add the ruler to the mix in Step 4, it absorbs some of the band's vibrations. You've made the length of the band shorter. The vibration of the shorter bands is faster, which creates a higher pitch. In Step 6 when you move the ruler to one side or the other you now have a piece that's shorter and a piece that's longer. The longer lengths make sounds that are low and kind of heavy sounding because they vibrate more slowly, giving a slower rate. The shorter side of the rubber bands make higher, shorter sounds. These move at a faster rate, known as frequency.

EXPERIMENT 3

HOW DOES LIGHT TRAVEL IN AIR?—A light experiment

Things you'll need:

You'll need 3 or 4 index cards and a pencil. You'll need some small pieces of modeling clay or some type of sticky tack so you can stand up the cards. You'll need a good quality hole-puncher that can punch a small-sized hole. You'll also need a ruler and your science journal. Working in a dark room helps too so you can see where the light is traveling.

What to do:

Step 1: Take the index cards and use your pencil and the ruler to draw the diagonals. The purpose of this is to locate the center of each of the cards.

Step 2: If you've done Step 1 correctly, you've identified the center of each card. Now you can use your hole-puncher to punch a hole in each card at the center.

Step 3: Use your modeling clay or tack to create a "stand" for each card so that you can position them upright on a tabletop.

Step 5: Turn the lights off in the room and flash the flashlight through the holes.

Step 6: Record your observations in your science journal.

What this experiment shows:

If you set up your experiment correctly, you'll see that the light travels through the holes in a straight-line path. What do you think would happen if you made the holes in your index cards smaller?

HOW DOES LIGHT TRAVEL IN DIFFERENT MEDIUMS?

A light experiment

Things you'll need:

You'll need a sizable glass jar and access to a water source. Your jar should be large enough so the ruler can fit inside. You'll need a cup of vegetable oil, a spoon, and a ruler.

Step 2: Using a spoon gently pour out the oil a spoonful at a time. It should form a surface layer of oil on the top of the water in the jar.

Step 3: Put the ruler gently into the glass jar through the oil and water. You should be able to observe the numbers on the ruler.

Step 4: Place the ruler in different positions to observe the way the numbers and lines on the ruler appear.

What this experiment shows:

Your previous experiment showed that light traveled in a straight line in the air, but in different mediums it bends. This is the effect you're seeing when you notice the numbers appear stretched or larger as if they were magnified.

EXPERIMENT 5

THE RAINBOW SPINNER—A light experiment

Things you'll need:

You'll need some white cardboard and some markers.
You'll need scissors, a pencil, and a small electric motor.
You'll need something like a compass or a template to
draw a large circle.

What to do:

Step 1: Using the template or compass draw a 5-inch circle on your cardboard.

Step 2: Divide the circle into seven sections and fill each section with one of the colors of the rainbow in this order: red, orange, yellow, green, blue, indigo, violet.

Step 4: Using the pencil poke a small hole in the center of the circle.

Step 5: Attach the circle to a small electric motor so it can spin at the center.

What this experiment shows:

Light is made up of all seven colors in the rainbow. When you spin the spinner very fast the colors blend together and the effect is that you see the light given off as white.

SUMMARY

You've learned a lot about sound and light by performing these experiments. When you're setting up and performing experiments either at home or at school, make sure there's always an adult there to supervise. Write down what you think will happen before you start the experiment. Your prediction is your hypothesis.

Take notes in your science journal during the experiment. Did the experiment turn out the way you thought it would? Why or why not? You can then form conclusions about the experiment. By testing your hypothesis with an experiment, you're using the scientific method.

Awesome! Now that you've finished these fun experiments using sound and light, you may want to perform some experiments with food in the Baby Professor book Funny Food Experiments for Kids – Science 4th Grade.

HO
NH₂
CH₃
R·CH·NH₂
HO
N⁺
N
SO₃H
NH₂
Cl
N=N
CH₃

Visit
BABY PROFESSOR
EDUCATION KIDS
www.BabyProfessorBooks.com
to download Free Baby Professor eBooks
and view our catalog of new and exciting
Children's Books